Goats
For Kids
Amazing Animal Books
For Young Readers

By Rachel Smith
Mendon Cottage Books

Mendon Cottage Books

JD-Biz Publishing

Download Free Books!
http://MendonCottageBooks.com

Table of Contents

Introduction

Did you know that goats won't eat just anything? They're actually very picky eaters. This is in spite of many sources showing them eating everything from homework to tin cans.

Goats are very interesting creatures; they have been domesticated (herded and raised by humans) for longer than people have had a written language. Goats aren't a bit part of modern day life for most people, but they have long been a source of food, clothing, and other goods for people the world over.

Goats are good for milk, fibers (to make fabric out of), skin, meat, and their horns. They are similar to sheep in a lot of their uses to humans, and it's no wonder, because they're cousins.

Domestic animals include dogs, cows, sheep, cats, and horses; the goat is one of many. However, they are unique among their fellow domestic animals in many ways.

What are goats?

Goats are probably one of the earliest animals domesticated (made friendly to humans). We can never know for sure, since there are no records of early caveman times, but along with the horse, the dog, and the cat, goats were made friendly to humans early on in time.

They are the source of protein for many people throughout the world, and there are more goats in China than in anywhere else in the world.

A goat and a kid in a meadow.

Goats are a cloven footed animal, like the camel and the pig. That means their feet are split down the middle. A goat is a member of the *Bovidae* family, which mainly consists of goats and antelopes. They are closely related to sheep. Most goats are descended from a goat in the *Capra* species, and come from mostly Eastern Europe, Asia, and Africa.

There are different kinds of goats. A female, grown-up goat is called a nanny goat or a doe, and a baby goat is called a kid. A male grown-up goat is called a buck or a billy goat, and a male who can't have kids is called a wether.

Beyond that, there are many different breeds, over 300. Goats can be anywhere from small pygmy or dwarf goats to 300 pound boer giants. Most goats are around the same size, however, which is closer to the size of a larger dog.

Goats and humans

Goats were domesticated thousands of years ago. Humans have used them for food and goods since then.

A boy feeding a goat.

Goats are typically kept in herds, and in countries that aren't industrialized, are usually watched over by children or teenagers. They wander the hills and graze throughout the day. This method has been used for thousands of years.

In America and Europe, goats are usually kept in pastures, which are fenced in areas. In the winter, they are kept housed in stables, where they can be kept warm. Also, in America and Europe, goats are usually kept in two varieties: for meat and for milk. Does are kept close to the milking shed if they are milk goats; if they are meat goats, it doesn't matter where they roam as long as they stay in the pasture.

Goats are also kept as pets, especially small goats such as pygmies or dwarves. Kids are often very fun to watch, jumping around and climbing everything.

Goats were first brought to America by Christopher Columbus, the explorer who discovered America; now, there are millions of goats worldwide kept by humans, though most of them are in Asia and Africa.

What do goats eat?

Goats are picky eaters. The reason people think that they will eat anything is that they will *try* anything. However, what goats will eat all of is entirely different from what they will try.

A goat eating grass.

While goats will eat grass, they much prefer bushland. They like to eat plants we call weeds, as well as plants like alfalfa and hay. Goats don't like eating anything that's dirty; this is where they're most picky. If it tastes bad or has mud on it, a goat won't eat it.

This is because goats are herbivores, which means they only eat plants. Sometimes they are mistaken for omnivores, which means they will eat anything; this is not true. Goats are pickier than their cousins the sheep or the cows.

Goats also need salt in their diet. Like deer, they enjoy a good salt lick, and if they don't have salt then they won't be healthy. It's also very important for goats to have clean water, because they don't get enough water just from the plants they eat alone.

Grain is also a good source of food for goats. A lot of farmers who keep goats will use it to feed their herd, though they'll use separate kinds for milking nanny goats and kids and bucks.

Like cows, goats have four-chambered stomachs, which is a bit similar to having four stomachs. It's because they have to get all the nutrients (the good parts) out of their food.

Goats can never eat azaleas, which are a kind of plant. It's poisonous to them, and will make them very sick.

Goats and their appearances

As far as animals go, goats are a bit unusual in how they look. They are cloven-footed, which is not uncommon, and they have different kinds of coats (hair), from curly looking angoras to shaggy coats to short coats. Goats do not have fur; they have hair, which can be used for clothing and other goods.

Nanny goats have udders with two teats, which is what the kids drink from.

Goats also have horns, which are used to fight each other. However, if they're kept by humans, they're often dehorned (their horns are removed) so that they don't hurt each other. It's a similar idea to getting cats declawed.

The most unusual thing about the goat's appearance is its eyes. Goats have a horizontal (sideways) pupil, which looks like a letterbox slit. Goats can also sometimes have blue eyes, though more often they have a yellow/gold color or brown. It's said that they had great night vision, and will often use this night vision to eat at night.

Goats often have floppy ears (though they also can have straight ears) and a split upper lip. Their upper lip is prehensile (meaning that it can grab things), and they use it to explore their environment. That is why goats will nibble at anything: it's their way of finding out what something is.

A goat's eye.

Only human males can have a beard (usually), but female or male goats can have a beard. It is a fluff of hair underneath their lower jaw, though not all goats have it. They may also have a wattle, which is a piece of skin covered with hair that hangs from the chin or neck.

They also don't have teeth on their upper front jaw; this means they don't have any big front teeth like humans do. Goats also don't have tear ducts, which means that their eyes don't water like humans.

They are quadrupeds, which means they have four legs. Most goats look a lot alike, though as said before, they can vary a lot in size.

They look a little like their close cousins, sheep, and their other cousins antelopes, but goats have an appearance all their own.

How do goats act?

Goats are social creatures. They live in herds, like their cousins, sheep. Nanny goats give milk to their babies for about two to three months, though a kid has already started eating grass and weeds at about the age of two weeks or so. Bucks aren't very involved in parenting.

They tend to spread out, instead of clumping together like sheep. Nanny goats don't watch kids very closely, which can lead to trouble.

Butting heads is a way that goats fight, usually bucks for the sake of attracting does. They also do it for the sake of proving who's in charge. Usually, it's pretty harmless, though it can injure either participant or even kill them. Goats tend to be more likely to charge a predator or human than a ram; they are more likely to fight in general.

Goats are very smart. They often escape their pens, usually by jumping over or ramming the gate until it breaks. They are far more likely to escape their pens than a sheep would be.

They hate to get wet. Goats will almost always try to find something to stand under when it rains. This is because their coats can get moldy if they get too wet and don't dry out.

The sound a goat makes is called a bleat, and they can range from small sounds to loud screams. A goat can even sometimes sound like it is saying a word, though no goats can speak like a human or a parrot.

One thing that's also very interesting about goats is their amazing balance. Goats can balance far better than humans, and can even climb some trees. This is one of the ways that goats get out of their pens. They can balance in ways that might even be impossible for a human. Sometimes they even stand on cows or humans. There's a reason for the phrase 'Surefooted as a goat'!

Goats also love to jump, and can jump as high as 5 feet. They're known for frolicking (or jumping around for fun), especially as kids.

Most goats breed seasonally, meaning that only at certain times of the year will a doe get pregnant. However, this often depends on the climate; if it's a mild climate all year round, or the breeders make the right conditions, then breeding may happen any time of the year.

As for gestation, which is how long a nanny goat is pregnant, goats take about five months until they give birth. It depends, however, on the breed; smaller goats take less time.

A nanny goat can have 1 to 6 kids, though usually she has less than four. By a few months old, a kid will be weaned off of their mother's milk. Does can keep producing milk for a year or more so long as the farmers continue to milk them. A kid is mature at about six months. That's a far cry from humans.

Pygmy Goats

Pygmy goats are on the small side in the goat world. They are common in Africa, and could best be described as being shaped like a short sausage with legs. They aren't shaped quite the same way as other goats.

A pygmy goat.

They were introduced to America as a pet in the 1950's, from zoos in Europe. They have become quite popular as pets, and are about 50-80 pounds in size. They are some of the smallest goats in the world.

Pygmy goats are typically kept as pets, but they can also be used for meat and milk. They live 8-18 years, so it's no small investment to get a pygmy goat.

As pets, Pygmy goats are very friendly, as well as resilient. Most goats are fairly hardy. They are some of the most common animals kept in petting zoos.

They can adapt to any climate, which makes them a very good pet for anyone with enough space.

Australian Goats

Australian goats are large in number. They were brought over when Australia was first settled by the British, as a source of food. The interesting thing that has happened with Australian goats is that a lot of them escaped from their pens or were set free in bad times. Now they live in the wild in herds in Australia.

It was around the turn of the century that this happened. Now, Australia not only has a massive rabbit problem to deal with, but also a goat problem. Goats are well used to clear land of shrubbery, and so they do the same thing in Australia.

The problem is that goats are not native to Australia, and they don't necessarily have natural predators. That means that they grow bigger and bigger in number without anything stopping them.

There are similar goats living in Scotland, who were set free during bad times. However, they are far more native to the area and not the same problem as the Australian goats.

Domesticated Australian goats, however, are good for their hair, their meat, and their milk, and are a good business in Australia.

Boer Goats

Boer goats have white bodies and brown heads. They are also one of the bigger breeds of goat. They can weigh over 300 pounds, making them enormous compared to their tiny siblings the dwarf and pygmy goats.

Boer goat.

Boer goats are probably descended from native goats in South Africa. The word Boer is a word that was used to describe a farmer in South

Africa before the British settled there; the name was used for the goat because farmers raised it.

This kind of goat is raised for its meat. It's not common for them to be used for milk or for their hair. Large groups of boer goats are raised in America in Texas.

American LaMancha Goats

American LaMancha goats, also known as just LaMancha goats, are the only American-developed breed. Mrs. Eula Fay Frey is the one who registered the breed, and she had the first goats called LaMancha.

They've only been a breed since about the 1950's, which is very new in the world of goats.

American LaMancha Goat.

LaMancha goats are some of the stranger looking breeds. Their ears are incredibly short, and are known as either gopher ears (only one inch or less for the ears, plus almost no cartilage, the non-bone matter that makes up ears) or elf ears (2 inches or so for the ears, including some cartilage).

They also produce a lot of milk compared to the average goat, and their milk is high in fat.

Dwarf Goats

Dwarf goats are like pygmy goats, but they aren't shaped quite the same way. They're like smaller versions (kinds of) normal goats. They are also in Africa, like the pygmy goats. They can weigh about 20 pounds, usually.

An African dwarf goat on a farm.

Unlike Boer goats, dwarf goats are mainly milk goats. They were brought to the United States of America as food for big cats in zoos, but they caught on as hobby animals. People typically keep a few rather than a large herd, unlike big farms.

There aren't very many differences between dwarf goats and normal sized goats besides the size.

Landrace Goats

Landrace is a word that means native to the area. It means that the breed or species has lived in that spot as long as any trace can prove.

A pair of Dutch landrace goats.

There are several landrace breeds. These include the Dutch landrace, the Swedish landrace, the Danish landrace, and the Finnish landrace. All of these goats live in chillier climates, and as such tend to have longer hair.

The Dutch landrace, in particular, has very long hair. It is usually brown, white, and black in color. Landraces are the native goats of the Northern lands, which is unique because most goats come from Asia, Eastern Europe, and Africa.

Alpine Goats

Alpine goats live in the French Alps, a mountain range that is in France, but also extends through Switzerland and Italy. They have upright ears.

Alpine goats have long been kept by the people who live in the mountains; since the land is not the best for farming, goats provide a lot of the food.

They are great milkers, and the milk can be used for a lot of different things. From cheese to soap to ice cream, goat milk can be used for anything that cow milk can be used for, and it is less likely that someone will be allergic to it.

All goats have milk, but alpine goats are some of the best milkers.

Alpine goats can a lot of different colorings and markings. The French have many different names for the markings and colorings. For instance, cou blanc (which means white neck in French) can refer to a white front with black and brown markings on the head and backside.

Another example of a name for markings and coloring is pied, which means spotted. This term is also used for horses and ponies.

Angora Goats

Angora goats are a type of goat with a sort of curly coat. It looks sort of like the fleece of a sheep. It looks very shaggy and messy before it's been sheared.

An angora goat.

Angora goats' hair is used for fabric, and is called mohair. It is very soft, and is typically used to make things like sweaters and blankets.

They come from Turkey, which used to be called Ankara (or Angora, which is where the name comes from). This type of goat is kept mainly for its mohair coat, and is shorn twice a year.

They used to be on the reverse of a Turkish 50 lira note. Angora goats are fairly important in Turkey, though they are bred in many places in the world now, including Texas and Europe.

Cashmere Goats

Like angora goats, cashmere goats are prized for their hair. There are many different kinds of these goats, which live in places like China and India and have been brought over to other countries as well.

A cashmere goat.

The name cashmere comes from the place in India, Kashmir. It's there that the goats' hair started to be used to make clothes.

Cashmere is the second coat of a goat; cashmere goats, and all goats, have two layers. They have a bristly outer layer, which they have all year round, and then they have an under layer, which is soft and only grown for the winter season.

This is the layer that is harvested from cashmere goats. Like angora goats, they are kept in large herds and aren't used very much for milk or meat.

Mountain Goats

Mountain goats are not true goats. They are an American species, and they live high in the mountains, known as alpine or subalpine regions. They are as surefooted as a goat, and they look sort of like them, which is why they were named goats by European explorers.

A mountain goat and a kid.

They are related to goats, but not as closely as sheep. Mountain goats are interesting creatures, however, because they do seem a little like goats.

They butt heads, like goats. Females fight a lot, usually over food and other resources, though males only fight when trying to impress a female.

Cloven-footed, the mountain goat has dewclaws in its hooves. This means it has sharp little bits on its hooves to help it hold onto the mountain, which is important because otherwise they might fall off!

They live in the Rocky Mountains, as well as the Cascade Range, in North America. This means they live mainly in Canada and the United States of America.

Mountain goats, unlike true goats, have never been tamed. However, their wool has been used by the native population long ago when they would shed their winter coats. Mountain goats are wild animals, and they are much more aggressive (more likely to fight) than true goats. They would make very bad domesticated animals.

Conclusion

Goats are an interesting animal, from their prehensile lips to their head butting to their amazing balance. They also provide a great deal of food and clothing, especially in poorer countries. Goat milk is the most common source of milk (barring human milk) for people worldwide.

As the backbone of protein sources in many countries, goats are a valuable resource, and will continue to be so for as long as food is necessary.

Author Bio

Rachel Smith is a young author who enjoys animals. She's always wanted to get a goat of her own (preferably pygmy), as well as about a dozen cats and dogs. Once, she had a bunny who was very nervous. She's also had several pet mice, who were the funniest little animals to watch. She lives in Ohio with her family and writes in her spare time.

Download Free Books!
http://MendonCottageBooks.com

Purchase at Amazon.com
Website http://AmazingAnimalBooks.com

Horses
For Kids

Amazing Animal Books
For Young Readers
By John and
Annalee Davidson

Ponies
For Kids

AmazingAnimalBooks

Rachel Smith

Ten Amazing Horses
For Kids

Nature Books for Kids
JD-Biz Publishing
K. Bennett

Akhal-Teke
"The Golden Horse of the desert"
For Kids

Nature Books for Kids
JD-Biz Publishing
K. Bennett

Suffolk-Punch
"The Gentle Giant"
For Kids

Nature Books for Kids
JD-Biz Publishing
K. Bennett

Shires
"The great Horse"
For Kids

Nature Books for Kids
JD-Biz Publishing
K. Bennett

Colonial Spanish
"Horse of the Americas"
For Kids

Nature Books for Kids
JD-Biz Publishing
K. Bennett

Canadian
"The Little Iron Horse"
For Kids

Nature Books for Kids
JD-Biz Publishing
K. Bennett

Cleveland Bays
"History and Future"
Horses For Kids

Nature Books for Kids
JD-Biz Publishing
K. Bennett

Our books are available at

1. Amazon.com

2. Barnes and Noble

3. Itunes

4. Kobo

5. Smashwords

6. Google Play Books

Download Free Books!
http://MendonCottageBooks.com

Publisher

JD-Biz Corp

P O Box 374

Mendon, Utah 84325

http://www.jd-biz.com/

Mendon Cottage Books

P O Box 374, Mendon Utah 84325

Made in the USA
San Bernardino, CA
01 November 2016